THE HEARTSTRING

PARIZA NAZIR

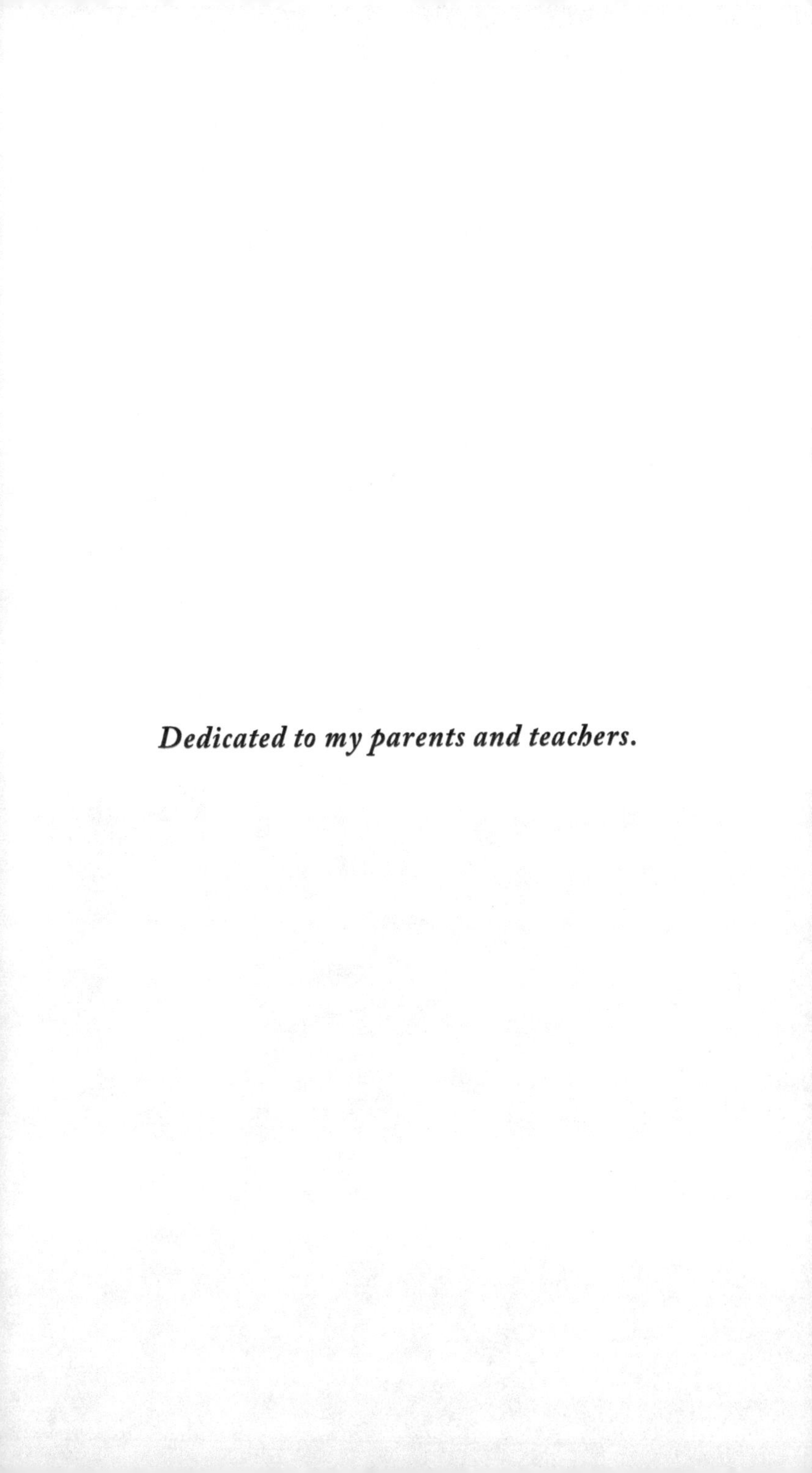

Dedicated to my parents and teachers.

Contents

Contents

Contents

Acknowledgements

Writing a book is not a solitary endeavor, and I am deeply grateful for the support and encouragement of so many people throughout this process.

First and foremost, I want to thank my Aadil Ghulam Bhat for his unwavering support and encouragement. My teachers, their love and belief in me have been a constant source of strength and inspiration. I am especially grateful to my parents for their patience and understanding during the many long hours spent writing.

I am also indebted to my beloved teacher Mr. Sharif Murtaza who had provided invaluable feedback, insights, and encouragement along the way. Their support has been instrumental in shaping this book and bringing it to fruition.

I want to express my deep gratitude to my editor and publishing team for their guidance, expertise, and belief in this project. Their dedication and hard work have been essential in making this book a reality.

I am also grateful to the many teachers, mentors, and role models who have inspired me over the years. From mindfulness and meditation teachers, their work has laid the foundation for this book and helped to shape my own approach to personal growth and transformation.

Finally, I want to thank the readers of this book. It is my hope that it will serve as a source of inspiration, guidance, and support as you navigate your own journey of personal growth and discovery. Thank you for your willingness to explore new ideas and perspectives, and for your commitment to creating a more fulfilling and meaningful life.

About Author

Pariza Nazir
25 February 2011

Pariza Nazir is a splendid and determined understudy at present concentrating on in Class ninth at Smart Mission high School in Gassipora Wanpoh, Anantnag. Brought into the world on February 25, 2011.

Pariza hails from (Laram Ganjipora) Anantnag and is the loved little girl of Nazir Ahmad Mattoo.

Pariza has always been a voracious reader and an enthusiastic participant in school activities. She is known for her enthusiasm for learning and her inquisitive nature. Her scholastic process has been set apart by her obligation to greatness and her longing to investigate new skylines. Pariza enjoys creative writing and has a keen interest in storytelling in addition to her academic pursuits. "A Bad dream" denotes her initial endeavor into the universe of writing, where she dives into the domain of dreams and fears, winding around a story that charms the peruser's creative mind. This book was written by Pariza as a result of her own experiences and vivid dreams, which have always intrigued her. Through her composition, she plans to interface with her perusers, offering them a brief look into the intricacies of the psyche mind and the undertakings that unfurl inside it. With the backing of her family and her mentor, Pariza keeps on taking a stab at significance in her examinations and her imaginative undertakings. Her excursion as a youthful creator is simply starting, and she anticipates imparting a lot more stories to the world.

1. Unanswered Prayers

I sought you in every prayer, my plea sincere,
Yet, you were not destined to be near.
Each supplication, each bowed head,
For you alone, my wishes pled.
Thus, each prayer remained in vain,
For my heart sought only your gain.
Had I prayed with love for the Giver's grace,
Perhaps today, you'd hold my place.

2. In That Gathering

I spoke of you in that gathering's light,
In words so vivid, your presence bright.
Their yearning eyes sought you so,
They asked for examples, not knowing where to go.
How could I explain, where to start?
For what example could match your heart?
A beauty incomparable, beyond compare,
In every way, a wonder rare.

3. Daily Quest

I meet everyone in your city with glee,
Imagining you in each face I see.
Feeling your scent in the air,
Seeking you here, seeking you

4. The Hopeful Journey

Hoping to chance upon you on a path anew,
With that hope, I set out each day too.
Each day you do not appear,
I console myself, tomorrow you'll be here.

5. In Your Absence

After parting, what joy did you find?
Was there anyone who loved you as blind?
Even in your absence, my love remains,
Seeking your sight in all my pains.
In my every good deed,
I seek the reward of your sight indeed.

6. Faithful Heart

They ask why I stay apart from the world,
As if they do not know, my heart unfurled.
My world is complete in my solitude,
For it's there I find my soul's latitude.

7. Restless Wanderer

You made me used to your sight so fair,
Now, like a mad man, I wander everywhere.
Seeking a glimpse, a trace of you,
In every alley, my search is true.

8. Without You

Every moment without you feels like a sentence,
How could you leave, causing this penance?
You said live long as you bade goodbye,
But even in your farewell, a curse did lie.

9. Broken Promises

They once promised, without you, they'd not survive,
Empty oaths, empty words, just to thrive.
What was their aim, what did they gain?
Even as they left, their words were vain.

10. Love's Betrayal

What did I endure in love's name,
Defamed, faithless, bearing the blame.
What answer will I give on judgment day,
For the sins committed in love's sway?

11. In the Gathering

Everyone was present in that gathering fair,
Yet, without you, it felt bare.
They asked what sorrow I bear,
How could I tell, our souls were a pair?

12. Seeking You

I roam the streets seeking a sight of you,
For everywhere, I look anew.
How can I explain, how can I say,
That you are within, every day.

13. . Unspoken Pain

How can I express the pain of your absence?
Neither words nor tears can convey its essence.
My eyes plead not to stay wet,
But how can I bear more, with my heart's fret?
Perhaps my eyes will tire someday,
And in place of tears, red drops will sway,
Death might come as I shed my final tear,
Expressing my heart's sorrow clear.

14. An Invaluable Gem

How could I ask you to stay?
You'd ask, by what right do I sway?
How could I tell, an invaluable gem I placed,
In your care, my heart embraced.
What could you say, what could you do?
My life in your hands, it's true,
How could I tell, you're my life, my all,
Taking my life, as you depart, I fall.

15. A Faithful Heart

They say, what holds you so tight,
That your heart doesn't stray in their sight.
I reply, my heart is true,
It won't change its direction, without you.

16. Dreams and Reality

17. The Scar of Your Betrayal

You seemed a precious flower in my heart's garden,
Your false loyalty seemed fragrance, a begotten pardon.
But the thorn of your company pricked so deep,
As if it stole my soul, my heart did weep.
Your betrayal left my heart barren,
Neither garden nor flower, just empty terrain.

18. Like Zulekha

My state is like Zulekha's, longing in pain,
While you, like Yusuf, forget me again.
I wander the streets, seeking a glance,
While you've forgotten our past romance.

19. Seeking Clues

When they say they've seen you, I yearn anew,
And gaze into their eyes, seeking a clue.

20. Divine Love's Mercy

O God, your love was truly grace,
A method for Adam and Eve's repentant embrace.
You favored their repentance, indeed,
When they invoked your beloved's name, they were freed.
In their repentance, you turned their plea,
Into a melody of love, sung by thee.

21. Yearning for Divine Union

To attain divine recognition, thus I pray,
Longing for a glimpse, in such a way,
As Jacob sought peace, his heart in a spin,
Waiting for Joseph's embrace, akin.

22. . Parted But Not Forgotten

If you have parted ways from me, yet not in disdain,
True, you're not here in life's domain,
But in my dreams, you remain,
Always mine, without refrain.

23. Tangible Love

How could I have known, dear,
Your love was a rare flower, near.
In my heart's garden, it did bloom,
But your betrayal brought a gloom.
Your thorn pricked deep, it stole my peace,
Your love was no flower, just a fleeting lease.

24. Devotion's Grace

Your love, a unique grace, I declare,
Not found in any worldly affair.
The joy of being your devotee,
Surpasses all earthly royalty

25. Yearning for your presence

Thinking you are my own,
I yearn for a moment when you'd be mine alone.
In this hope, I find my stay,
Longing for you every day.
Each night, restless with memories of you,
My heart aches for a rendezvous.
Your absence turns me into a patient,
Needing your sight as my healing agent.
With such deep desire, I keep my vow,
For you to cure me with your presence now.

26. The Precious Gift

To every prophet, you granted a wonder rare,
But it seemed your beloved was left with nothing to bear.
Yet, when the Kalima was proclaimed,
Your name was seen with his name framed.
Then your beloved believed true,
No other received a gift so precious from you.

27. Flower and the Nightingale

Once my mother told me so,
"Like a flower, my child, you grow.
With the truth of your character bright,
The whole world will bask in your light."
You are like a flower, pure and sweet,
And they, like a nightingale, in your presence complete.

28. Flower and the Nightingale

Once my mother told me so,
"Like a flower, my child, you grow.
With the truth of your character bright,
The whole world will bask in your light."
You are like a flower, pure and sweet,
And they, like a nightingale, in your presence complete.

29. Longing for Reunion

I have no business with Gabriel's flight,
Yet I yearn for our words to unite.
Though my deeds may not be grand,
Still, with desire I stand.
I wish my greetings to reach my friend,
With whom my words have long ceased to blend.
To win back that dear one, I strive,
For nothing else do I contrive.

30. Endless Wait

How much longer must we yearn in vain,
How much more must we endure this pain.
Let us cease this endless wait,
Let us finally see you, our hearts elate.

31. Love Story's Tale

People marvel at my love story's tale,
They say, "What came to ruin you, hearing it, did not
fail."
I smile at my state,
Would they relieve my heart of your memories' weight.
Swearing by your name...

32. Fragrance of Presence

I meet every soul in your town with eager delight,
Imagining, when with them, I sense your presence bright,
Feeling your fragrance in the air, so light.

33. Last Meeting

For ages, the image of our first meeting has been
Etched in my eyes,
Now, let's frame the picture of our
Last meeting in these eyes.

34. Last Meeting

*For ages, the image of our first meeting has been etched in
my eyes,
Now, let's frame the picture of our last meeting in these
eyes.*

35. Same Street

By chance, we crossed paths on that single road,
Since then, longing to see her has become my ode,
Thus, I wander the same street, my heart's abode.

36. Priceless Gifts

The treasures you gave me,
I keep close with tender care,
From the flowers intertwined with thorns,
To the falsehoods in your words' rare,
From the fleeting beauty of moments you shared,
To the wounds from your silent stare,
My love,
From the shattered pieces of my heart,
To the fragments of memories we dared,
For I cherish these gifts as priceless,
Carrying them with me everywhere.

37. Solitude's Twilight

For you, I've forsaken even the light's glow,
You meet me in the quiet of night's show.
What can I do in these crowded gatherings bright,
When you only meet me in my solitude's twilight.

38. Morning Breeze

The morning breeze arrived with your message in tow,
Bringing the essence of your presence, a gentle glow.
Your fragrance carried, it reached me so near,
And returned the smile to my face, oh so dear.

39. World in Solitude

They ask why I sit so far from the world's sway,
Asking why I choose solitude, day by day.
But how can I explain, in what way?
That my world is found in my solitude's stay.

40. Eternity's Show

How did you manage to forget me so,
Is it even possible, how could it go?
I couldn't forget you, no matter the flow,
It's beyond possible, till eternity's show.

41. Jasmine's Gate

For ages, I've been beholding her from afar,
Longing for so long to be her confidant, a star.
But oh, wretched fate,
As I approached her, the jasmine's gate,
Someone was keeping me distant, an unyielding state.

42. Quiet Gathering

We sat quietly in the grand gathering,
They said, "Why are you sitting so melancholy?"
They asked if you were lost in thoughts of her, why so sadly?
We replied, there's nothing of that sort,
Just quietly sitting here, no more to report.
When they spoke of you in that assembly,
Our lips faltered and became empty.
And silence and sadness quietly took over,
Somewhere in the depths, hidden in clover.

43. Trembling

When I see you in the mirror, I speak to you,
Why do my lips tremble so, it's true.
When I write your name with my pen's ink,
Why do my hands tremble, what do you think?
When I hear your name spoken aloud,
Why does my body tremble, so proud?
Oh, why am I like this, why so consumed by you?

44. Beyond Might

I could look at him, but he's nowhere in sight,
What could I do,
It wasn't within my might.
Now, in dreams, I could see him clear and bright,
Yet he never lets me sleep tight,
It wasn't within my might.

45. Heart's Unrest

To whom can I confide the state of my heart's unrest,
Who will recall the one entrenched within my chest,
Who will tend to the wounds inflicted by your hand,
Who comprehends my intense yearning for you, yet
unplanned?

46. Enchanting Creator

I'm amazed to think that our existence began with a glance,
glance,
Crafted with such effort, every detail in advance.
Hence I ponder, the entity that laid this foundation,
How enchanting must be the creator upon inspection

47. Why Have You Brought Me Here?

Oh God, by inflicting torment on me,
Why did you bring me to this misery?
How long will this spectacle continue here,
If you had to send me, why this despair?
You could have made me part of another being,
Instead, you sent me here as the highest being.
Thus, you bestowed upon me another plight,
Neither from that world nor this, I find light.
So why am I present in this place,
Oh God, tell me, in this case,
By inflicting torment on me,
Why did you bring me to this misery?

Conclusion

As we reach the end of this poetic journey through "Heartstring," we reflect on the emotions, experiences, and insights that have been woven into each verse. This collection has been a labor of love, an exploration of the deepest corners of the human heart, and a testament to the resilience and beauty of our shared humanity.

Through these poems, we have traversed the landscapes of joy and sorrow, love and loss, hope and despair. Each piece has been a thread in the intricate tapestry of life, capturing moments of vulnerability and strength, intimacy and isolation. The words have served as a mirror, reflecting not only my own experiences but also the universal truths that bind us all.

"Heartstring" is more than just a compilation of 46 packed poems; it is a celebration of the emotional spectrum that defines our existence. It is a reminder that, no matter how disparate our journeys may seem, we are all connected by the invisible threads of our shared emotions. These poems have sought to resonate with your own heartstrings, to evoke memories, and to inspire introspection.

In a world that often moves too fast, poetry provides a space to pause, to feel, and to connect. I hope that this book has offered you moments of reflection, comfort, and a sense of connection to something greater. May the words within these pages continue to echo in your heart, long after you have turned the final page.

Thank you for allowing "Heartstring" to be a part of your life. May you carry its essence with you, finding beauty in the ordinary and strength in the midst of adversity. Remember that every heartstring, no matter how fragile, contributes to the symphony of life.

With gratitude and hope,
Pariza Nazir

The End

*Is life just as a constitutional machinery, ticking
away with rights and duties?
Or is there a preamble to our dreams and
amendments for our hopes?
Maybe it's time to draft a new bill! for happiness.*

~Aadil Ghulam Bhat.